AF443831

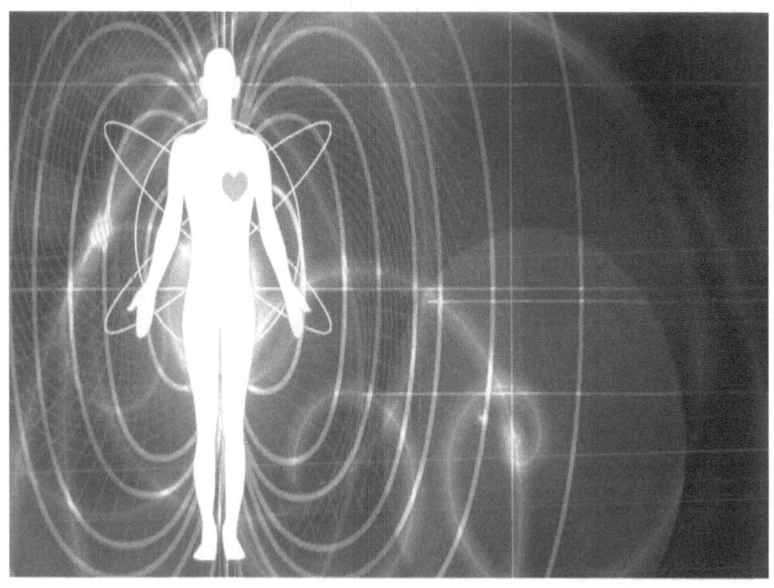

INTRODUCTION

Welcome to this collection of slices of modern life, as seen and experienced within the hopes and confines of urban living. What is the collection? Technically it is a set of prose poems (short, lyrical stabs of fiction) and poetry. This categorization aside, this book takes a surreal, slightly distorted look at life and, from this Lynchian perspective, perhaps sees the world more as it actually is as opposed to the fragmented vision presented through the 'prism of the mainstream.'

Please note that U.S. spelling is used throughout.

Maybe this is absurdist fiction? Surrealist? Does it strike a note of familiarity? All of these? There is certainly a strong note of dark humor.

You'll either find the tales in here funny, or you won't.

Judge for yourself.

Tim Sandle

For comments, clarifications, and requests for more of the same: pseudomonas@btinternet.com

Contents

SANCTUARY

The technician, noting the time that had slipped away from the glowing, green fascia, put down the assortment of wires and circuits he had been toying with. He moved purposefully to wash the yellow stain from his hands, before heading quickly out of the laboratory, hardly pausing to throw his white coat down onto a nearby bench.

He hurried past the silver, cylindrical towers close to The Company, which were sluggishly puffing grey, twisted curls into the pale blue sky. In order to make faster progress he moved sideways down an alleyway and proceeded to crisscross around a network of corroded pipes, which were connected to an out-moded chemical exhaust.

Moving back onto the main road, he reached the security gates, breathless. He handed over his plastic card to the visored security guard. The guard took the card, and without speaking, inserted it into a small slot in the wall. There was a flash of colored light, accompanied by a shrill electronic hum, as the gates opened.

He was met by a vast, overlapping network of concrete roads. The man rushed through, and nervously waited for a break in the traffic. It came, eventually, and he reached the other side and moved through an opening between two grey, tarnished metal blocks.

To a casual observer, the new location was not particularly different from the sterile, slabs of concrete and metal factory, with its towering geometric walls, where he spent ten hours a day. The technician stood on a spot marked with a red cross, about one quarter of the way down the center of a pale, grey rhombus. The rhombus itself surrounded by tall, metal walls which almost screened out most natural light. Surrounding the walls were a network of roads, carrying businesspeople and military people to and from irrelevant destinations.

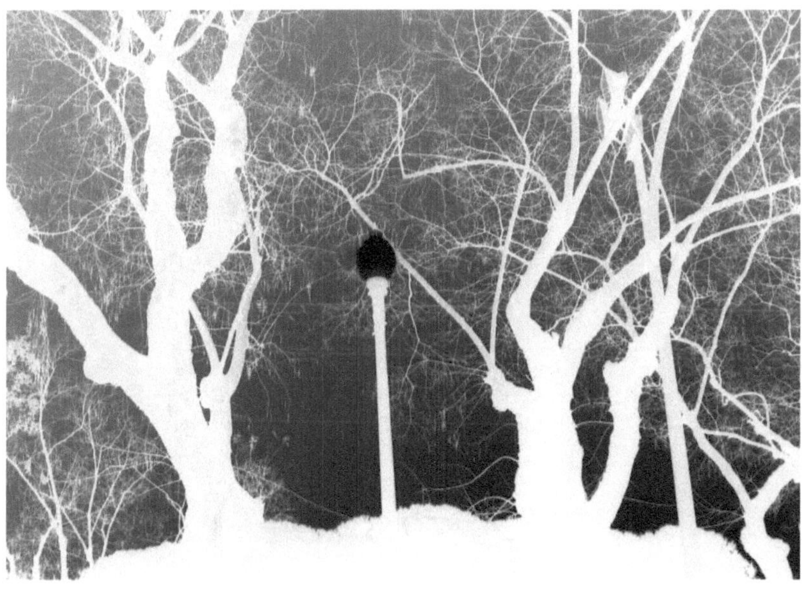

The surroundings, the movement of vehicles, was unimportant to him. The one solitary object, fixed in the center of the rhombus, was the only item in the world that interested him. He sauntered slowly towards it, enjoying the anticipation, the buildup. His heart began to beat rapidly. Had it changed? Had it grown?

He reached the small tree and smiled. He gazed, childlike at the green leaves, the partially formed buds, the intricate twigs, and knotted bark. He was content. At peace. This was his sanctuary. His shelter. His turn to look. A chance which came once every three or four years, to experience the last national treasure.

The alarm on his wrist chronometer started buzzing obtrusively. It was time to return to work.

GOING TO THE SALES WITH THE NEIGHBORS

Peering through the curtains on a cold, dank and dark morning I see that they have the car revving. As I wipe away the condensation, I see that it is a new one. A blue Sunnybeam family estate packed with Mr., Mrs., teenage girl, young boy, and Great Aunt Edna. It would ordinarily be a funny site. The squashed arrangement of the lower middle class. Funny, that is, if I didn't have to squeeze my bulk in between them.

The shopping trip I don't want to go on.

Fortunately, it isn't a long journey. A short chug into the big town and its big department store. We have to queue for a while with other similarly dressed people with the same half bored half-expectant looks on their faces.

Once the doors eventually open, we are attracted by a colorful sign proclaiming, 'Bargain Sale'. Like one swift animal we glide over towards it. A unified sigh: no real reductions so we glide swiftly back to find some other quarry.

We have better luck in the clothing section. Artfully arranged piles are quickly scattered. Airy pastels become mixed up with scarlet and black scarves. We all gape. The canny nosed woman, the bleary-eyed man, the bored little boy, the fashion intoxicated teenager all leer at the same stripped box.

A woman pushes through and burrows under a mass of woolen and synthetic fabrics. Deeper, deeper, deeper. Then jerkily out, with a scowl. They haven't got her size. Then a smile as she scoops up a fury garment and holds it tight in her plump clutches. Eyes, reinforced by tight lips, blaze at her.

I move on past assorted hand painted pottery with no history to another ordered pile being thrown into a state of confusion. I stand back this time from this microcosm of expression where the Chancellor's policy is played out with apparent spontaneity. I contemplate writing a manual, probably about thirty pages so it could be a pocketbook, with chapters headed 'Daring Reflexes', 'Eagle Eyes' and 'The Essential Refreshments To Take'. But I expect it would probably end up in the bargain bin. I glance at my watch. I'd better get moving.

After chugging back in the car more slowly I return, wearily, to my dark and cold flat. I spend a slow, regretful, and tiresome evening shifting through the bags and boxes of items I don't want. I suppose I'll use them as presents for next Christmas.

These jumpers will make nice gifts for the neighbors.

INSOMNIA

Bones aching, heart pounding,
Brain spinning, conjuring up images.
No drugs, no outside forces,
Alone. Trapped half-way here, half-way there.

Crunching, chewing, gurgling, coughing,
Too hot, too cold, too tight, too twisted.
Mistakes, errors, failings, pain
Fizzle and burn against my eyes.

Up shifting around, down lying still,
Sheet shackles, safety from the dark.
Sweat leaks, body clicks,
Shifting shapes corrode my mind.

Shivering, contortioning, scratching, sniffing,
Scared, relaxed, sad, comatose.
Pounding sounds, background tick-tucks,
Haunting cries for the passage of time.

CHERRY TREE LANE

There's a big town by a big river and the streets are fairly clean in this neighborhood. Look over there - a kid playing happily. I peer through a window and see a tall woman baking. I suspect her husband will be home soon, after stopping off at the pub. I'm moving on, I don't like this area.

I'm drifting on through the town. It's a little boring, nothing to describe, I feel like dreaming. I can't remember what happened during the night. I'm lying on the street now and people are rushing past. The businessmen over there, they're moving the fastest. Some people are wearing overalls, others are smoking cigarettes. Some are cramped inside cars.

I'm now skipping casually down one of the bigger streets. It's less crowded now. I've reached the tallest building. It is grey with glass. It really towers above me, I'm not sure that I want to go in. Inside people are counting money, some are smiling.

I'm leaving this town. I'm going way past the river into the country. I've had enough of it. I want dirt and rain. I'll watch the animals trying to survive. I'll build a small cabin and grow my own vegetables. I'll live all on my own. Yeah, I think I'll stay here forever.

HAPPINESS

White bird flying upwards into the blue,
Wings hammering constantly against natural forces,
Content.
A shuffle amongst the green glaze,
Strong wings alter direction,
Target located: a flash of brown,
Almost content.
Hunger.

Swooping, pirouetting, diving,
White dot on blue; blue against white,
It pounces, grasping the animal in its vice.
Brown. Brown and red,
Food.
Flying free in the sky,
White bird flying upwards into the blue,
Content.

HOLIDAY TIME

He held the syringe lightly in the palm of his hand as if it were a small animal. The needle was blunt and covered in a smeary black-grey . It had probably been used by many others. He didn't care. Maybe yesterday, when he still clung onto some semblance of reality he might. But not now. That moment of clarity had passed, dissipating into the air.

The syringe fell onto the floor. He started shaking again.

A mild tremor convulsed from some point in his back, across his bony arms and into the tips of his grimy fingernails. He made a motion to scoop the barrel up. He couldn't grasp it. His fingers kept opening a closing against his will. He ran his sweating hand along the concrete, scraping the skin. Eventually he regained hold of the syringe. He sat on the pavement swaying from side to side, eyes blinking, rotating the syringe over and over. Soon his eyes became transfixed on the yellow bubbles from the slopping liquid inside.

He watched until the bubbles became no more and coughed hoarsely. He shifted to his knees and rolled up the sleeve of his grey tunic, exposing the white flesh lassoed around arched bone. He spat onto his arm and began to rotate the salty fluid with his thumb. Quickly, he inserted the needle

Digging deep into the flesh. The instant moment of pain as the rusty needle penetrates. Depressing the plunger. A small fortune, from a tiny phial, shot up, cascading through his veins like demented express train careening off the tracks.

He threw the syringe away, folded his arms, closed his eyes and waited. A warm glow eased through his willow tree frame, causing his fingertips to glow at first. His body reacted positively. It was like being wrapped in silk. He curled over and gazed at the yellow orb above. He was happy. His yellow glow comforted him.

The pain was sharp and sudden. Pulsating. Scraping every nerve cell at once. It didn't last long but left him in a cold quiver. His consciousness began to ebb back.

He realized he was alone, engulfed in a blanket of silence. The second attack lasted longer. It penetrated deeper. After that he was too weak to move.

It was the fifth which finished him physically: obliterating most of his nervous tissue. His eyes continued to gaze up. He could no longer think. A shattered shell. In time his eyes failed to move, remaining, wrapped around the bobbing yellow.

ESCAPE

Spiraling upwards, tumbling downwards.
Gracefully across the powder blue sky.
Alongside billowing white cotton tufted clouds.
Fast, fleeting, feeling elated

Downwards in a smooth arc,
Edging past a tall, pointed tree.
Tickled on all sides by waves of sweet-smelling
green.
Crisp and welcoming.

Falling further down. Becoming darker.
The golden orb has shimmered from site.
Lower, to the gnarled, knobbed, twisted roots.
Feeling uneasy on the dark brown earth.

Little eyes glow, tempting.
Dull and wet.
Float up, quickly, past the tree,
Back to the tufty clouds, free.

ATOM

A void, a panorama of beckoning blue-blackness stretching out to nowhere. A distorted dimension in which future, past, present, all of time, is meaningless. There is no sense of physical movement. Just black, blue and nothing.

And then something. A small glowing point of light flashing briefly. Ten again. Slightly larger. Coming closer. Getting bigger. Glowing, globe like, spinning. A mesmerizing sphere of radiant light. Shining up the morbid darkness until it fills up the entire field of vision. So warm. So, comforting. Drifting away. Getting smaller.

Now a planet. Crude in shape. Angular and sharp. Crushed and ravaged surfaces on a softly glowing green buckled shell.

Retreating. Backwards. Now it is a twinkling star. A pin prick in a black box. Now, finally gone, only inky-blue blackness remains. Surrounding. Resembling home.

TIME FOR A CHANGE

He decided he needed a personality. Better than watching sitting around all day, he reasoned, slurping his tea.

So, he began by turning the TV news on every night and started studying the faces. He upgraded to films a week later. He recorded - on a big sheet of yellow paper - when people became angry, or jealous, or were in love, with the approximate times of the day that these emotions took place.

Yet he couldn't draw any worthwhile correlations. He attempted, and this required immense concentration, to re-enact facial expressions. He linked these to certain trigger words, such as, "that's nice, dear". Phrases that he could use in social situations, like bus queues or greeting the woman in the local shop.

He also sought to develop appropriate expressions without embarrassment. A greater range than he possessed before, allowing him to react more appropriately, should certain situations arise (or to his embarrassment, occur again).

He still felt dull, thinking about all of this. Could he really reinvent himself? Transform from the mundane to position of splendor? Shine with the stars or the cat's eyes in the road?

So, he started filling his head with facts. Crisp, clear, enjoyable facts. Some to make people laugh, others to make people stop and think. Perhaps one or two to make others cry.

To do this he drew up several methods, sketching these out on a big sheet of yellow paper (the kind that is ruled, but where the lines are quite short – is that called feint, he wondered).

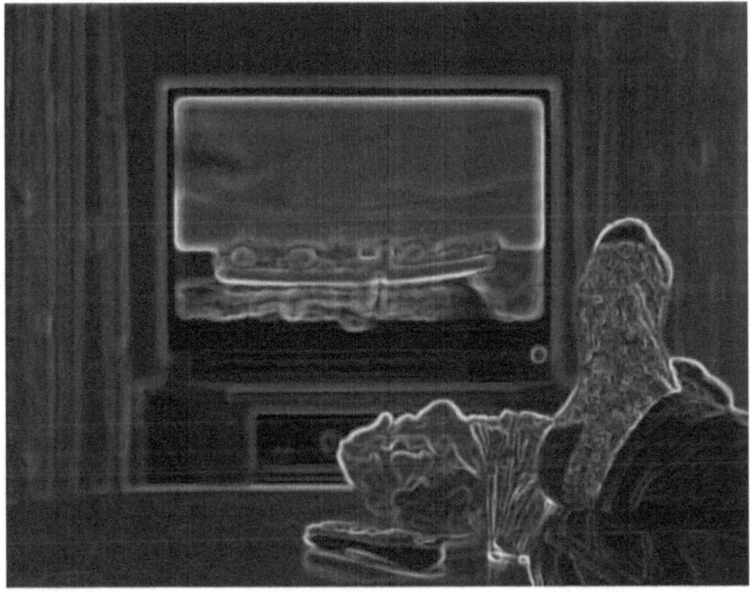

He would also only use pencil. A thick pencil, not too blunt. HB would be good, sufficient graphite for the task. Perhaps he'd write until he reached the stub. Sharpening his mind as he sharpened the lead...not that pencils contain lead, just a form of solid carbon.

The first attempt involved staring at people, trying to read their thoughts, but this proved mainly unsuccessful although older people were better because they tended not to notice. One thing he didn't like was a hostile reaction.

Secondly, he got hold of some cast-out X-ray prints, but he couldn't decipher them.

Finally, he read books on subjects he didn't like, hoping that the resistance to the content would generate extra brain capacity. He gave up with a headache when carrying out a study into magnetohydrodynamics.

He made one last attempt.

So, he began to dress up like famous people, and develop aspects of their lifestyle from magazine articles. He became obsessed with finding out the favorite food of celebrities because he had future social parties in mind. Also, if he eat like them then he'd start to understand them better. He knew he couldn't become them, that was a faintly ridiculous notion.

By this time, his head hurt all the time. He believed it was his brain growing. I don't know, he certainly knows more than last month. So, don't judge him harshly. He's happy. I guess.

HAVING A COLD AT CHRISTMAS

Being shoved, bustled, pushed, and trod on, especially when one is of a delicate nature, is not the most pleasant of experiences. It is made even worse whilst trying to carry heavy bags and suffering from a sore throat which feels like two abrasive sheets of sandpaper constantly being rubbed together.

Having a cold, and having to go Christmas shopping, is a problem for most people. I accept that. But because I'm here, right now, swishing around these damp suburban streets then no one has ever suffered as badly as me.

It is through some genetically implanted sense of duty that I venture out on the last shopping day (or is it a social construct? I skipped that class).

My nose is almost constantly blocked, functioning like a disused mine shaft which every so often displays a trickle of its wealth by oozing its contents down onto my cracked and salty lips.

At the moment the zip on my jacket is stuck and it has got to the point, despite the drizzle, that I can't be bothered with it anymore. It has made my head spin as violently as a plate in a Greek tavern.

A small woman has just bustled past me, tapping into my torso as she completes her seasonal mission. She's carrying an assortment of gifts wrapped in shimmering blue and silver paper. Almost fully loaded, about to double or drop.

Now she is now blocking my progress, filling her large frame within the sock aisle. I attempt to cough politely but the result is a hoarse splutter as fluid bubbles up to the back of my throat.

I try to clear my throat, which dislodges some of the mucus down into my stomach. Instantly my throat seems to become recoated with the foul-tasting slime.

My nose is running again but my tissue is now in tatters, loosely linked together chains of paper, no longer layered. Useless. Dry in some places, wet in others. I casually deposit the used tissue between two packets of yoga socks. Who wants socks for yoga anyway?

I abandon my quest to circumnavigate the underwear section. Not much else here. Time to move on, zapping from excessive heat, to the chill outside, and then bravely into another store for another unmissable retail experience.

Making my way into a different shop I sneeze at the change of temperature. It is now especially hot and stuffy, but no less crowded. On reaching the counter I discover that I am out of luck: no size seven's left

"They'll be in after the New Year", says the assistant curtly, her left eye giving me a flash of her disdain.

Inwardly I've crumbled. I feel like shouting and stamping except it would cause me too much pain.

I have had enough. I glance in a mirror by the over-sized dresses. Perhaps it is the artificial light, but I look a wreck. My yellow tinged skin, greasy hair and wide eyes reflected back.

I've decided to go home and shovel aspirin down my phlegm-ridden tunnel and forget Christmas shopping this year.

I'll buy them all bottles of wine. Online.

RE-TELLING AN OLD ONE

Imagine the scene, dear reader. This is a TV show, broadcast just gone midnight. Called 'Eerie Tales'(actually 'Unheimliche Geschichten', as there is a degree of pretentiousness about the proceedings, all shadows and sounds, a dribble of Gothic camp).

The show is introduced by Wilfred Wright, professor of Greek Archaic History, but we'll have to assume he is moonlighting here. Nothing better than getting an academic to front this kind of show ,it adds a hint of credibility. At least that is what the junior producer thinks.

In the role of the presenter, the storyteller is smoking a cigar (this is a 1960s recording, don't worry about modern sensibilities being offended). Our Dr. Wright is dressed in a crushed velvet jacket. The rain drizzles on the windowpane (or is that a sound effect?) There's the odd bolt of lightning too, and a crash of thunder. Effects designed to invoke a feeling of spookiness.

It's a black and white film, Saturday is crossing into Sunday. A half-an-hour of classic broadcasting from the BBC archives. One last program to watch before bedtime. You think that this is going to be good...

Onto our show, if you don't mind Wilfred.

Thud! He turned sharply, jumping a little. His anxious eyes stared forwards at the broken, knotted branch he had just clumsily snapped. The wind was increasing in pace. He paused besides a tombstone, shivering. "Keep calm", he murmured to himself, not very reassuringly. "You'll find your way."

He moved on, pulling his scarf tighter around his neck and stumbled on half-way into the graveyard. The moon was full overhead, casting wide beams down upon the tombs, capturing them in a soft, silvery hue. Some of the inscriptions were readable, all of the graves were old, pointing to the remains of those who had been interned during the late nineteenth century.

It was getting close to 10 o'clock. He was hungry and thirsty and had been walking for almost an hour. The sojourn from the railway station to the pub had not seemed very far, twenty-minutes he had reasoned when he'd looked at the map.

A large gust of wind threw up a cluster of dried leaves around his ankles. He moved on, quicker, through the narrow weedy paths which separated the graves.

After a few minutes he stopped, staring at one of the stone crosses in front of him. Shivering, he pulled the collar of his jacket up, and held his threadbare scarf more tightly around his neck.

Peering hard, he read the inscription, frowning. He passed this particular spot only a few minutes ago. He cursed himself for having taken this supposed shortcut.

"Can I help?" muttered a soft, pleasant voice from behind. He swung around with a nervous hop.

A man stood in front, dressed in a smart, slightly worn brown raincoat. He wore a tatty cap and his face had a weary, sanguine look. The man repeated his question in his syrupy rich tone, and then, eliciting no response, ventured.

"My name is Caskill. I live nearby".

Our protagonist took a moment to gather his composure. "Yes, er, yes. I'm trying to find my way through to Hammond's End. I'm supposed to be staying there tonight".

Caskill paused and smiled. "This way", he continued to beam, and swung his arm up, pointing westwards.

They moved together through the craggy graves, slippery grass, and in and out of the twisting trees, until they reached a small hedge with a narrow gap in the center.

 Caskill halted. "Go through the gap, keep close to the trees, turn left at the brook, and you'll be on the road to Hammond's End".

He smiled, relieved. "Thank you. That was a maze. Which way are you headed? I'd like to buy you a drink."

Caskill shook his head, so he persisted.

"Come along. It's cold. Have you been here long?"

Caskill frowned and scratched his brow. "To be honest I'm not sure how long I've been here".

"Then come!" He urged, moving towards the gap and gesturing.

Caskill remained still and spoke slightly hoarsely, his voice a little fainter than before. "Tell me. Do you believe in ghosts?"

He shook his head. His previous nerves had dissipated, as his thoughts were geared towards sipping a pint of beer. "No, of course not."

Caskill smiled. "That's good. Neither do I."

With that Caskill faded away into the darkness, leaving him alone by the hedge and under the grey sky.

For some reason, Wilfred really likes this film.

WAR SONG!

The last wisp of soft, grey smoke curled upwards
towards the clear, blue sky.
Bitterly, I tossed aside the bent stub.
As I hobbled faster to keep up with the others,
I lowered my hand on my knee feeling the soft
and soggy trickling red.
My gun was heavy, the strap dug deep into my
shoulder,
But I marched on with my burden strapped to my
back.

We were all wan, weary, woeful,
Dreaming of home, not of battle.
Sweat was plastered over our dirt encrusted faces,
We resembled shriveled grapes drying under the
sun.

The sun, hanging like a dinner gong, shone
stronger,
Sucking the juices from our mouths,
As we continued to saunter along the dust beaten
track,
Slumping, meandering, in torn, mud cased
uniforms,
Even the officers, who once modelled themselves
on lions,
Wandered and swayed with heads hung low.

I paused by a chipped rock,
An inviting refuge for my tired mind.
I flicked my eyes upwards at the blue sky,
I was the first to see it, but we were all too late.

A loud grating noise filled the air.
Some of them did not hear it, it did not really
matter.
The sky became a river of orange, floating down
upon us like a silk coat.
Surrounding, engulfing, seizing life,
As we fell to our knees, grasping our throats as the
boiling, bubbling sea of froth engulfed us.

They came for our bodies two days later,
Throwing our twisted and disfigured frames,
Into the back of a battered truck.
They were people like us, young, some still
innocent.
Next week they would be marching along some
other forgotten road,
Until the sky lit with sun colored vapor,
Or until someone actually says "stop".

HAWK

The white tail twitched. It blinked an eye. A pause, then with one swift leap it launched itself and circled high into the sky. Within a few fleeting seconds it had cleared the valley, a few moments more and it cleared the hills. An ever-purposeful streaking arrow.

With its wings slightly crooked back it hovered, almost motionless, glass eyes scanning. Suddenly, without warning, it appeared to freeze. Eyes locked upon the far away ground. A small climb higher and then a rapid decent.

Gaining in speed and focused upon the object below it released its scissor sharp professional claws. Closer and faster. Impact. The talons became hooked into the creatures back. The small animal stiffened as the beak snapped its neck. Slow down as the warm, rich red soaked carcass is devoured.

Satisfied, it raised its head and sprung back its legs, rising again into the grey sky. Within seconds it was gone. Neither the hawk nor the valley floor retained any memory.

LOVE

I was so miserable,
Two slugs slithered and slimed over my ear lobes,
I tore up the tacky tabloid,
Then I met you.

You lifted me up,
You were like the Sun: glowing, shimmering,
enchanting.
I felt put back together.

Then you left me.

LIVING TODAY

A politician's face on the TV screen...clothes in a
magazine,
That image in my head from that book,
I want to look like that...it's good,
They say so.
I know the ways to behave(drink that cola),
It's due to that style of music.

What my friends say...The picked up from the
papers,
Everything: music, fashions, moods,
What's out. What's in,
It must be good, they say so,
It's all around me. I can be an individual.

Interlude

A selection of ten photographs taken by Tim Sandle

Image 1: Gargouille

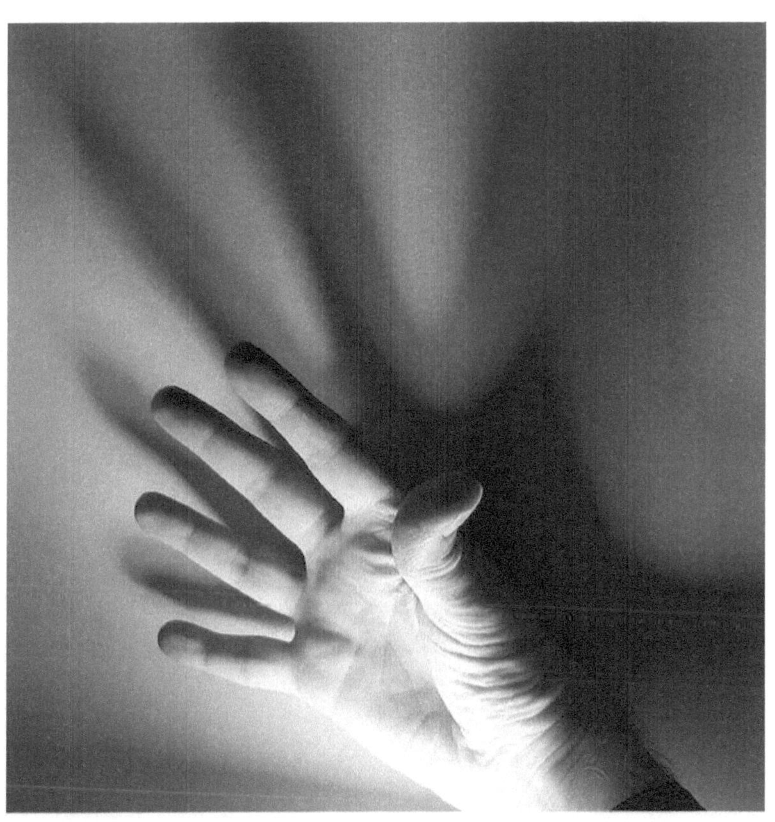

Image 2: Main fantôme

Image 3: Rue oubliée

Image 4: Cris et excitation

Image 5: Un endroit hanté pour se reposer

Image 6: Attention à ne pas frapper à cette porte

Image 7: Le crâne joyeux d'un homme mort

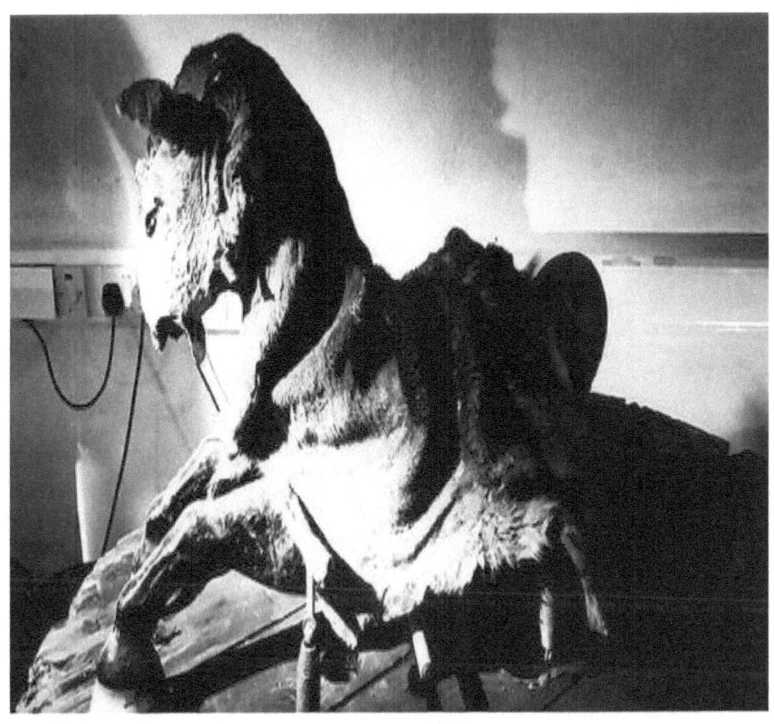

Image 8: Un jouet qu'il vaut mieux éviter la nuit

Image 9: Une femme autrefois noble gelée pour toujours, pour l'éternité

Image 10: Des volutes fantomatiques sur un champ abandonné

INTERNAL

They stop, together, two, but linked as one,
She is armed, clothed in black, potent,
He is restless, edgy, sharp.
A high-pitched scream reverberates; she fires the
gun.

They walk on, further into the dark,
There is no end, only darkness, hanging
oppressively,
And hidden eyes and extended claws.
The nervousness, anticipation and desire
culminate: FEAR.

Tension tightens like an over-wound clock,
A movement! Somewhere in the dreary, dank
darkness.
He cries out: PANIC.
She fires, and again, continually. There is noise.

She finishes. The noise has ended. He smiles,
She grins back, enigmatically, eyes wide,
Before stepping away into the black,
The comfort fades with her. He is alone. Darkness
all around.

OPERATION

She opened her right eye slowly, the lid flickering, causing his eye lashes to swish up and down. Distorted shapes twitched momentarily before blending into one. She gradually opened her left eye and the shape began to vibrate before blending into smooth, black blot. She opened and closed her eyes rapidly, in quick succession. Yet the blackness remained draped in front.

She repeated this action with his eyes again, before giving up.

Her brain ached through pumping confused thoughts; her eyes were strained and felt heavy. So very heavy.

Several minutes eased by before she slowly began to think. She could not understand why she could see nothing, of why she could feel nothing - no cold, no heat - of why she was there. A few more minutes cranked along and her head began to ache more from bone to tissue. It did not last for long. She lapsed into the arms of unconsciousness, without having solved anything.

ATTRACTION

A kind of soft Christmas red blazed in front of her. She hobbled a couple of steps backwards, the torn sole of her left trainer flapping. She could feel the intensity of the heat tickling her face. Creeping orange flames danced and twisted from both sides. She stared deep into them in wonder, looking at shapes, imagining shapes. In time the bobbing dance had surrounded her and crept upwards, towering above like tormenting giants. Taunting as they edged nearer. She stared back, unafraid, eyes wide, thrilled.

Her back was hurt first when the searing heat lurched forward like an inflamed tongue. Crackling little orange and red daggers glowed
pleasantly upon denim. Soon the shifted together and quickly spread over her whole body. A few short seconds and she was inflamed, still fascinated for her last few seconds, as she went up in a brief, orange, if not remarkably interesting, candle of flames.

OUR PROBLEM

Erm, I'm so terribly sorry. I made a mistake. I made a mistake. A rather terrible error, but we had a laugh later. It was a bad investment you see. I didn't calculate the crash. Several millions lost. I can afford it, maybe others can't. I shouldn't really care. No one would if it were me.

Yet why am I being criticized from all sides? All these people from the street - I've done enough for them; tacky tabloids; jealous colleagues? Mistakes are all part of being alive. I accept it. Everyone makes mistakes. The boy folding leaflets may miss one out. That's a mistake. The level of mistake doesn't matter, does it?

An image of the author

MIRROR

Yes. I can see you. Do you know that? I suppose I still love you. If I'm capable of that anymore. I keep trying to communicate with you. I'm concentrating really hard, pushing myself in all directions, to all corners. I'm trying to utter some noise, but nothing is happening.

It's so cold, so lonely. I feel de-centered. The only pleasure, if I can still feel that the same way, is watching you. Where are you going? Wait...please. Not the light, not darkness again.

I'll wait. What is time anymore? How long have I been like this? When did I physically die?

How much longer must I spend in total darkness or gazing at the same green, chipped walls? The wooden bed, with its creased and twisted duvet, and the pile of clothes on the floor. The same images reflecting into me, day after day.

So, I'm here. Covering this expanse. I feel the cold and the hot. I experience the night and the day. I know you. I love you. But I cannot switch off the images. I'm a permanent voyeur gazing at a one act play in a continued state of wakefulness.

Some time ago I felt this alternative to death was heaven. To still be able to see you. To see you living out your hopes and fears.

Now you're moving. Hauling great boxes filled with our things. There goes the bed. Nothing left but me. Now me. Don't forget me. Don't leave me.

Nothing. Alone.

Aphorisms for a time and place

Aphorisms almost always come from life experience. They're passed on from someone who's "walked the walk." These aphorisms are general remarks on life: the good, the bad, and the ugly.

* A barking dog never bites.
* Absence makes the heart grow fonder.
* All that glitters isn't gold.
* An ounce of prevention is worth a pound of cure
* Children should be seen and not heard.
* Doubt is the beginning, not the end, of wisdom.
* East or west, home is best.
* Eat to live; don't live to eat.
* From the sublime to the ridiculous is but a step.
* Genius is one percent inspiration and 99 percent perspiration.
* Ignorance of the law is no excuse for breaking it.
* Imitation is the sincerest form of flattery.

- Possession is nine-tenths of the law.
- The more things change, the more they stay the same.
- The proof of the pudding is in the eating.
- The race isn't always to the swift, nor the fight to the strong, but that's the way to bet.
- You can lead a horse to water, but you can't make it drink.
- You can't fight city hall.
- A penny saved is a penny earned.
- All things come to those who wait.
- Don't hide your light under a bushel.
- Don't judge a book by its cover.
- If you do what you've always done, you'll get what you've always got.
- Know which side your bread is buttered on.
- He who pays the piper calls the tune.
- Measure twice cut once.

Lockdown lament

It was nice when it started.

Taking a break.

No people around.

Alone.

Quiet, and able to get on with things.

To do what I want.

To go where I want (at the start, not anymore).

Mask on, gloves on.

Keeping a distance.

Now it is dull.

Endless days.

Same old, same old.

Everything has been tidied up.

Life sorted out.

So quiet.

Waiting for the end.

Mask is frayed.

The distance is too far.

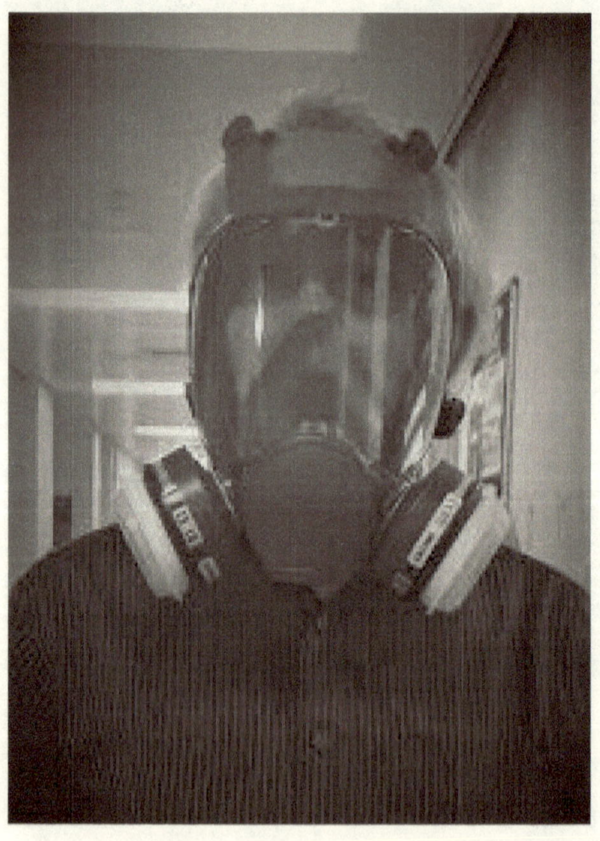

Cathode Ray Tubes

Used to be so bright.

Now clapped out, burnt out.

Toxic and unwanted.

Once so popular, broadcasting to a nation.

Black and white images transferred with sound.

Wavy lines and UHT.

One way to get the BBC.

Showing Gothic films and phantasmagoria.

Tall tales at children's teatime.

Of witches, giants, and toys coming to life.

Flickering images signaling the start of the night.

What remains?

There's some in a museum.

The guy down the road still has one.

It takes five minutes to warm up.

He can give it a bang, if he has no luck.

Yet when it starts,

Then he can enter into the world of worlds,

The world of imagination.

The End.

Thank you for reading.